CH
F

GW01072128

by Heather Morris
Illustrations by Peter Lawson
Cover by Peter Lawson

Nightingale Press
Bath

Copyright © 2006
Illustrations © 2006

First published in the UK in 2006 by
Nightingale Press
Bath BA2 3LR
All rights reserved

Reprinted 2008

Produced in the UK
Printed in Malta

13 digit ISBN: 9781903056 23 3
       ISBN: 1903056 23 3

"At no other time has Nature concentrated such a wealth of valuable nourishment into such a small space as in the cocoa bean."

Alexander von Humboldt, natural scientist in South America in the 1800s

AZTEC ORIGINS

The botanical name for cocoa is "Theobroma Cacoa" meaning 'Food of the Gods'. The ancient Maya Indians and the Aztecs used cocoa beans both as an ingredient for 'xocolatl', a bitter frothy drink flavoured with chilli, and as currency. The drink was highly prized and often served in golden goblets. Emperor Montezuma allegedly drank 50 goblets a day.

CURRENCY

Aztec taxation was levied in cocoa beans. You could buy a rabbit for 4 cocoa beans, the services of a prostitute for 10 beans and a wife or a medium quality slave for 100. Counterfeiters used to drill small holes in the beans and fill them with earth.

SPANISH SECRET

The Spanish Conquistador Don Cortes was the first European to popularise chocolate. When he returned to Spain in 1528 he brought back cocoa beans and equipment for making the chocolate drink. Chocolate became a fashionable drink enjoyed by the rich in Spain where it was a closely guarded secret.

SHEEP'S DROPPINGS

English and Dutch sailors, who found cocoa beans in the Spanish treasure ships captured as they returned from the New World, failed to recognise their importance. The precious beans were thrown overboard by angry sailors who thought they were 'sheep's droppings'.

CACAO OR COCOA?

It was as a result of a misspelling that **cacao** became **cocoa** throughout the English-speaking world. Cacao is still used to refer to the tree that grows the melon-shaped pods which contain the beans. Technically, they are cacao beans, but they are known throughout the chocolate industry as cocoa beans.

HARVESTING COCOA

Cocoa is normally harvested twice a year and every tree produces about 3-4kg of beans annually. All the work is still done by hand and the pickers use long handled knives that can reach the highest pods and snip them without damaging the soft bark of the tree. It takes about 400 beans ground up to make 500g of chocolate.

FERMENTING COCOA BEANS

Every fruit contains 25 to 30+ almond sized beans which are fermented for five to six days. The fermentation process kills the germ of the bean which becomes porous and brown, the bean's aroma develops and makes it suitable for chocolate manufacturing. The beans are then left to dry for one to two weeks.

ROASTING THE BEANS

Next the dried and fermented beans are roasted for 10 up to 30 minutes at a temperature of 120-130C (250-265F), in some cases slightly less. The roasting process is extremely important as it has a huge impact on the final flavour of the chocolate.

GRINDING AND PRESSING THE BEANS

Before the cocoa beans are ground the husk and germ are winnowed away. At this state the beans are called cocoa nibs. Then the nibs are ground into a paste called cocoa mass (or cocoa liquor or paste). The paste is pressed in a hydraulic press which extracts at least half the fat to create cocoa powder. The extracted fat is cocoa butter.

EUROPEAN CRAZE

It took nearly a century for the news of chocolate to spread across Europe. The Dutch finally broke Spain's monopoly of cocoa beans when they captured Curacao. Cocoa was acclaimed in Holland and recommended by doctors as a cure for almost every ailment. It first arrived in England in the 1650s when it became very popular in the court of Charles II.

QUALITY CHOCOLATE

The quality of chocolate varies enormously. The best will contain:
- *56-70% cocoa solids, to include 31% cocoa butter*
- *29-43% sugar*
- *1% lecithin and pure vanilla extract*

The best cocoa comes from Criollo beans. These used to be the main source of cocoa but they are now only 4% of world production.

MASS-PRODUCED MILK CHOCOLATE

A standard recipe for this would be:
- *11% cocoa solids*
- *3% vegetable fat*
- *20% milk solids*
- *65% sugar*
- *1% lecithin and synthetic vanillin*

> *"Chemically speaking, chocolate really is the world's perfect food."*
>
> *Michael Levine, nutrition researcher*

HOT PUDDINGS

STEAMED CHOCOLATE PUDDING

Serves 4-6
- *90g self-raising flour*
- *120g soft butter or margarine*
- *30g cocoa powder*
- *120g caster sugar*
- *2 eggs*
- *90g plain chocolate, grated*
- *1.5 litre microwaveable bowl, greased*

- *Beat together the flour, butter, cocoa, sugar and eggs.*
- *The mixture should be a soft dropping consistency - add a little milk if needed.*
- *Stir in the grated chocolate.*
- *Transfer to bowl and cover with cling film.*
- *Pierce cling film and cook at full power for 4 - 5 minutes depending on power of oven.*
- *Test with a skewer - it should come out clean.*
- *Stand for a couple of minutes before serving with custard or cream.*

EATING CHOCOLATE

Originally chocolate was always served as a drink. Fry's and Cadbury's produced bars for eating but these were dry, crumbly and not very tasty. The introduction of the van Houten cocoa press in 1866 was the real breakthrough as cocoa butter, extracted from the cocoa beans, is the essential ingredient for eating chocolate.

SWISS MILK

In 1875, a Swiss manufacturer, Daniel Peters of Vevey, produced the first milk chocolate bar using powdered milk. Peters switched to using Henri Nestle's condensed milk which produced a superior taste and texture and the two men founded a company to manufacture the first milk chocolate.

CHOCOLATE QUEEN OF PUDDINGS

Serves 4
- *285ml milk*
- *90g caster sugar*
- *2 x 5ml spoons cocoa powder*
- *30g butter*
- *60g white breadcrumbs*
- *2 eggs, separated*
- *Greased pie dish*

- Preheat the oven to gas mark 4, 180C, 350F.
- Heat the milk, 30g sugar, cocoa and butter in a saucepan.
- Put the breadcrumbs in a bowl and pour on the milk mix.
- Allow to cool slightly then stir in the egg yolks.
- Pour the mix into the pie dish and bake for 30-35 minutes.
- Whisk the egg whites until very stiff and fold in the remaining sugar.
- Pile the meringue on top and cook for a further 10-15 minutes until pale golden and set.

"There are four basic food groups: milk chocolate, dark chocolate, white chocolate, and chocolate truffles."

Anonymous

DARK AND WHITE CHOCOLATE

Dark, or plain, chocolate has no added milk. European rules specify a minimum of 35% cocoa solids but high quality brands will contain around 70%. White chocolate is based on cocoa butter without the cocoa solids. Purists don't believe this should be called chocolate and some popular 'white chocolate' bars don't contain any ingredients from the cocoa bush at all.

CHOCOLATE FONDUE

Serves 2
- *1 vanilla pod*
- *300ml whipping cream*
- *500g dark chocolate*
- *brandy or Grand Marnier (optional)*

For dipping in the fondue
- *fruit such as strawberries, banana, kiwi, grapes, apple slices*
- *marshmallows*
- *walnuts or brazil nuts*

- *Split the vanilla pod and scrape the seeds into a heavy saucepan or fondue pot with the cream and heat gently.*
- *Melt the chocolate in a bowl set over hot water.*
- *When the chocolate is melted pour into the cream and stir well.*
- *Keep hot but do not overheat.*
- *Add a dash of liqueur if desired.*
- *Use cocktail sticks or small skewers to dip.*

PEARS IN CHOCOLATE

Serves 6
- *6 ripe dessert pears*
- *2 x 5ml spoons lemon juice*
- *75g caster sugar*
- *cinnamon stick*

Sauce
- *200ml double cream*
- *150g light brown sugar*
- *25g unsalted butter*
- *25g golden syrup*
- *120ml milk*
- *200g dark chocolate, in pieces*

- *Peel the pears keeping them whole.*
- *Scoop out the cores from the base and slice so they stand upright.*
- *Brush with lemon.*
- *Heat the sugar and cinnamon stick with just enough water to cover the pears and poach gently for 10-15 mins.*
- *Heat the cream, sugar, butter, syrup and milk gently until melted, then boil for a few minutes until thick.*
- *Remove from heat and add the chocolate, stirring until melted.*
- *Transfer cooked pears to serving dish and pour on the sauce.*

CHOCOLATE CHEMICALS

The mood-boosting chemical in chocolate is phenylethylamine, which it is found in much bigger quantities in some other foods like tomatoes and fruit. However, chocolate also stimulates the release of serotonin and endorphins, natural body hormones that generate feelings of pleasure and well-being.

CRAVINGS

15% of men and 40% of women admit to chocolate cravings. These are usually most intense in the late afternoon and early evening. At certain times of the month women need extra magnesium and, guess what, dark chocolate has a high magnesium count. In pregnancy, craving could indicate mild anaemia, which chocolate's iron content may help to cure.

HAPPY BABIES

Scientists in Finland say eating chocolate during pregnancy may make for happier, livelier babies. They questioned 300 women before and after they gave birth. They found those who ate chocolate daily were more likely to say they had active, happy babies who smiled and laughed a lot.

COLD PUDDINGS

QUICK CHOCOLATE TART

Serves 4

- *100ml double cream*
- *30g caster sugar*
- *pinch of salt*
- *60g soft butter*
- *230g dark chocolate*
- *60ml milk*
- *ready made pastry tart shell*

- *Bring the cream, sugar and salt to boil in a saucepan.*
- *Remove from heat and add the butter and chocolate broken into small pieces.*
- *Stir until completely melted and blended in.*
- *Allow to cool slightly then add milk stirring until mixture is smooth and shiny.*
- *Pour mixture into a ready baked tart shell, allow to cool then chill for 1-2 hours. Serve with cream.*

WOMEN AND SEX

According to Italian researchers, women who eat chocolate regularly have a better sex life. The study found: "Women who have a daily intake of chocolate showed higher levels of desire than women who did not have this habit. Chocolate can have a positive physiological impact on a woman's sexuality." But many women still claim to prefer chocolate to sex.

GOOD FOR THE HEART

Eating chocolate may help to keep the heart healthy. A European study suggests that polyphenols - which occur naturally in cocoa - appear to relax the blood vessels, making blood flow more efficient and reducing the strain on the heart. Dark chocolate can also boost blood antioxidant levels by nearly 20% protecting the heart and arteries from oxidative damage.

CHOCOLATE MOCHA MOUSSE

Serves 4
- *230g plain chocolate*
- *2 large eggs, separated*
- *40ml liqueur (Drambuie or Grand Marnier)*
- *40ml strong black coffee*
- *230ml double cream*

- *Break chocolate into small pieces and melt in bowl over simmering water.*
- *Stir until smooth. Remove from heat and cool slightly.*
- *Stir in egg yolks, liqueur and coffee.*
- *Whip cream until just floppy and gently add to chocolate mix.*
- *Whisk egg whites until stiff and fold in carefully making sure they are evenly blended.*
- *Pour into individual dishes, cover with cling film and chill for 2-3 hours.*

LONGER LIFE

A study of 8000 male Harvard graduates showed that chocoholics lived longer than abstainers. Their longevity may be explained by the high polyphenol levels in chocolate which can protect against heart disease.

100+

Two of the world's oldest supercentenarians Jeanne Calment (1875-1997) and Sarah Knauss (1880-1999) were passionately fond of chocolate. Jeanne Calment regularly ate two pounds of chocolate per week until her doctor persuaded her to give up sweets at the age of 119 - three years before her death aged 122.

CHOCOLATE BANANA TART

Serves 8-10
- *100g plain chocolate*
- *175g butter*
- *225g Rich Tea biscuits, crushed*

Filling
- *200ml creme fraiche or cream cheese*
- *2 ripe bananas, mashed*
- *1 x 5ml spoon lemon juice*
- *50g caster sugar*
- *2 medium eggs*
- *40g self-raising flour*
- *1 x 2.5ml spoon vanilla essence*

- Melt chocolate with the butter and stir in crushed biscuits.
- Press crust into baking tin.
- Bake at gas mark 4, 180C, 350F for 15 minutes.
- Beat cheese until smooth, then beat in bananas, lemon juice, sugar, eggs, flour and essence until smooth and thick.
- Pour filling onto crust, bake for a further 30-35 minutes until firm.
- When cool, decorate with cream and banana slices dipped in lemon juice.

CHOCOLATE PIZZA

A sweet pizza dripping with chocolate and mascarpone was marketed by a supermarket as an ideal Valentine's treat. It combined a chocolate base with sticky black cherry and chocolate sauce topping and was finished off with chocolate flakes and dollops of mascarpone.

CHOCOLATE DIET PILL

A British company is testing the effects of a cocoa-based diet pill that could soon be ready for launch on the US weight loss market. A spokesman said, "We will have a chocolate-tasting product that suppresses diet. People can take one tablet just before each meal to reduce their appetite. Now you can have your cake and eat it."

WHITE CHOCOLATE CREME BRULEE

Serves 6
- 5 large egg yolks
- 115g granulated sugar
- 480ml whipping cream
- 90g white chocolate, finely chopped or grated
- few drops vanilla essence
- 60g caster sugar
- 6 ramekins

- *Preheat oven to gas mark 2, 150C, 300F.*
- *In a large bowl whisk together the egg yolks and half of the sugar.*
- *Put the cream and rest of the sugar into a heavy saucepan and bring to simmering point.*
- *Reduce the heat and gradually add chocolate whisking until smooth.*
- *Remove from heat.*
- *Whisk the hot chocolate mixture into the egg yolks, add the vanilla and mix well.*
- *Pour into 6 individual ramekins.*

- *Place the ramekins into a roasting tin and add enough hot water to come half way up their sides.*
- *Bake for about 45 minutes or until the custards are just set in the centre.*
- *Allow to cool then refrigerate for at least 3 hours.*
- *To serve, sprinkle caster sugar over top of each custard and caramelise either by using a catering blowtorch or by placing under a very hot grill for 2-3 minutes.*

BALANCED DIET?

A Midland mother claimed she has survived on almost nothing but chocolate for 49 years. Chocoholic Cathy Creegan said she never eats a normal meal, but just bars of chocolate, spending up to £200 a month. 'The only other thing I eat apart from chocolate is potato. I can manage the odd bowl of mash or a couple of roast potatoes. I've always been like this, ever since I was a baby.'

DARK CHOCOLATE PAVE

Serves 8
- *300g dark chocolate*
- *275g caster sugar*
- *165g unsalted butter*
- *pinch of salt*
- *5 large eggs*
- *1 x 20ml spoon ground almonds*
- *icing sugar to dust*
- *20cm or 23cm cake or tart tin with removable base, buttered*

- Preheat the oven to gas mark 4, 180C, 350F.
- Melt the chocolate, sugar, butter and salt in a bowl over barely simmering water.
- Remove from heat.
- Whisk the eggs with the ground almonds and then fold gently into the chocolate mixture.
- Pour into the tin and bake for 35-40 minutes.
- Allow to cool and dust with icing sugar.
- Serve with cream or ice cream.

CAMEL'S MILK CHOCOLATE

Low fat camel's milk chocolate is due to hit the shelves after an Austrian chocolate maker joined forces with an Arabic camel farm. Camel's milk is a good alternative to cow's milk because it is lower in fat and sweeter. The chocolate is called Al Nassma, after the cool wind that blows in the desert.

VEGELATE

Bars made with cocoa and vegetable fats instead of cocoa butter are popular in Britain and many other countries including the USA. There was a campaign within the European Union for these to be called "vegelate" not chocolate, but this was fiercely resisted and, despite scare stories in the press, was never agreed.

DEATH BY CHOCOLATE

Dogs metabolise the chocolate ingredient theobromine more slowly than humans. Safe doses for us can be toxic or even lethal for our pets. A small bar of plain chocolate (100-150g) will be enough to kill an average sized Yorkie; a medium sized bar (200g) a spaniel; and a large bar (400g) a Labrador. Horses have also died from eating cocoa bean hulls used in bedding.

CAKES AND BISCUITS

EASY CHOCOLATE CAKE

- *60g cocoa powder dissolved in a little hot water*
- *230g soft margarine or butter*
- *4 eggs*
- *230g self-raising flour*
- *1 x 5ml spoon baking powder*
- *230g caster sugar*
- *2 x 18cm sandwich tins, greased and lined*

- Preheat the oven to gas mark 4, 180C, 350F.
- Put all the ingredients into a large bowl and beat well for 3-4 minutes using an electric mixer if possible.
- Divide the mixture between the tins and smooth out.
- Bake for 30-40 minutes until firm and well risen.
- Cool in tins for 5 minutes then turn out onto wire rack.
- Sandwich together with Chocolate Butter Icing.

CHOCOLATE BUTTER ICING

- *25g cocoa powder*
- *60ml boiling water*
- *250g icing sugar*
- *175g butter or soft margarine*

- *Dissolve the cocoa in the boiling water to make a smooth paste.*
- *Add the icing sugar to the butter or margarine and beat really well until the mixture is pale and fluffy.*
- *Stir in the cooled cocoa mix.*
- *This is enough to fill and decorate an 18-20cm sponge cake.*

SPA TREATMENT

In the Bayern health resort Bad Birnbach chocolate is considered a healthy treatment for the skin. They offer baths in chocolate, which moisturises dry skin and also leaves your body with a chocolate fragrance for several hours.

CHOCOLATE ORANGE CAKE

- *230g self-raising flour*
- *90g cocoa powder*
- *230g soft butter or margarine*
- *290g caster sugar*
- *2 large eggs, beaten*
- *240ml milk*

Filling and topping

- *230g soft butter*
- *grated rind of an orange*
- *230g icing sugar*
- *juice of half orange*
- *2 x 18cm sandwich tins, greased and lined*

- *Preheat oven to gas mark 4, 180C, 350F.*
- *Sift the flour and cocoa together.*
- *Cream the butter and sugar until fluffy then gradually add beaten eggs.*
- *Stir in the milk then fold in the sifted flour and cocoa.*
- *Put the mixture into tins and bake in centre of oven for about 35-40 mins until well risen and springy.*
- *Remove from tins after 5 minutes and cool on wire rack.*
- *When cool, split each cake carefully into two layers.*

- To make the icing and filling, cream together the butter and orange rind then beat in the sifted icing sugar and orange juice alternately, a little at a time.
- Sandwich all the layers together with the orange icing and use the rest to cover the top of the cake.
- Decorate with preserved orange slices.

"Strength is the capacity to break a chocolate bar in four pieces with your bare hands - and then just eat one piece."

Judith Viorst

CHOCOLATE ROULADE

- 90g caster sugar
- 5 medium eggs, separated
- 50g cocoa powder
- Swiss roll tin, greased and lined

Filling
- 300ml double cream
- 45ml brandy
- 50g caster sugar

- *Preheat the oven to gas mark 4, 180C, 350F.*
- *Whisk the egg yolks and sugar until thick.*
- *Sift in the cocoa and fold in gently.*
- *In a separate bowl, whisk the egg whites until stiff then fold into the chocolate mix.*
- *Pour into tin and cook for 20-25 minutes until well-risen.*
- *Turn out onto a board dusted with caster sugar and leave to cool.*

- *For the filling, whip the cream and brandy until it holds its shape then stir in the sugar.*
- *Spread about ⅔ over the sponge.*
- *Roll up carefully from the long side. It may crack.*
- *Decorate the top with the remaining cream.*

VEGETABLE?

In Denmark they reason like this: *Chokolade* is obtained from cocoa beans. Sugar is extracted from sugarcane. Both beans and canes are vegetables, so chocolate must be a vegetable!

CRISPIE CAKES

Makes 12-15
- *100g plain chocolate*
- *50g butter or margarine*
- *20ml golden syrup*
- *1 x 20ml spoon cocoa powder*
- *125g rice crispies, cornflakes or similar unsweetened cereal*
- *15 paper cake cases*

- Break up the chocolate and melt it with the butter, syrup and cocoa powder in a large pan over a gentle heat.
- Stir until smooth then carefully mix in the cereal.
- When completely covered in chocolate, spoon the mixture into the paper cases.
- Press gently so that it sticks together. Chill in a refrigerator.

VIENNESE WHIRLS

Makes 8-10
- 150g plain chocolate
- 350g butter or margarine
- 75g icing sugar
- 1 x 5ml spoon vanilla essence
- 60ml milk
- 350g plain flour
- 175g cornflour
- 1 x 2.5ml spoon baking powder

- Melt the chocolate over hot water.
- Cream the butter and sugar until pale, then add the melted chocolate, essence and milk.
- Beat in the dry ingredients until the mixture is really light.
- Using a piping bag, pipe quite deep whirls on a baking tray allowing room to spread.
- Bake at gas mark 5, 190C, 380F for 15-20 minutes.
- Leave to harden before lifting onto cooling rack.

WHO EATS THE MOST CHOCOLATE?

Switzerland leads the world in chocolate consumption with 16kg per person. UK comes second with 14kg. Austria and Ireland are not far behind with 12kg and 11kg, respectively. Americans consume 5kg per person but this adds up to almost half of the total world's production.

JAPANESE LUXURY

The best chocolate is sold in single pieces in Japan with the standard price being 300 yen (£1.50). The most expensive chocolates, containing foie gras, sell for 1,000 yen each. These prices don't seem to affect the appetite of Japanese shoppers, the most fanatical chocoholics outside Europe and America.

HOLLYWOOD BROWNIES

Makes 16
- *60g dark chocolate*
- *115g unsalted butter*
- *250g brown sugar*
- *2 eggs*
- *1 x 2.5ml spoon vanilla essence*
- *120g plain flour*
- *pinch salt*
- *250ml roughly chopped walnuts*

- Preheat the oven to gas mark 3, 165C, 325F.
- Melt the chocolate and butter in a pan over low heat stirring gently.
- Remove from heat and stir in the sugar.
- Add the eggs and vanilla essence while beating thoroughly.
- Stir in the flour, salt and walnuts and mix well.
- Pour into a greased baking tin and bake it for 40 minutes.
- Cool on a rack then cut into 16 squares.

CHOCOLATE CHIP MUFFINS

Makes 16
- *120g plain chocolate*
- *120g dark Muscovado sugar*
- *240ml milk*
- *60g butter, melted*
- *2 eggs, beaten*
- *290g self-raising flour*
- *1 x 5ml spoon baking powder*
- *120g white or dark chocolate chips*
- *muffin tins or paper muffin cases*

- Preheat the oven to gas mark 6, 200C, 400F.
- Melt the chocolate in a bowl over simmering water.
- In a large bowl mix the melted chocolate with the sugar, milk, melted butter and eggs.
- Sift in the flour and baking powder, folding in gently.
- Stir in the chocolate chips.
- Spoon the mixture into greased muffin tins or use paper muffin cases.
- Bake for 20-25 minutes until well-risen and firm. Leave in tins for a few minutes then cool on a wire rack.

ASIAN BOOM

With chocolate consumption increasing at a rate of 25% a year in the Asia-Pacific region, and 30% in China, chocolate makers fear that cocoa bean growers will not be able to keep up with demand. A new and unforeseen catastrophe presents itself: global chocolate wars.

TOKYO CELEBRATES

In 2002 a 3m tall chocolate statue of David Beckham was crafted out of 3,000 bars to promote the Meiji chocolate brand. To celebrate Mozart's 250th birthday in 2006, a chef created a chocolate sculpture of the score of his Turkish March studded with 107 diamonds. It was valued at 5m dollars.

NO COOK FUDGE FINGERS

Makes 12
- *230g digestive biscuits*
- *60g chopped nuts*
- *90g raisins*
- *115g plain chocolate*
- *1 x 2.5ml spoon vanilla essence*
- *30g cocoa powder*
- *1 x 345g tin of condensed milk*

- Crush the biscuits and mix with the nuts and raisins.
- Melt the chocolate, essence, cocoa and milk together in a bowl over simmering water.
- Mix into the biscuit crumbs.
- Press the mixture into a greased tin and chill for 3-4 hours, then cut into fingers.

SECRETS OF THE STARS

When Katherine Hepburn was asked about her longevity, she claimed it was due to, "A pound of chocolate a day, a healthy regular diet and plenty of exercise."

"After about 20 years of marriage, I'm finally starting to scratch the surface of that one (what women want). And I think the answer lies somewhere between conversation and chocolate."

Mel Gibson

CHOCOLATE CHIP COOKIES

Makes 16
- *100g butter or margarine*
- *200g plain flour*
- *1 x 5ml spoon baking powder*
- *pinch of bicarbonate of soda*
- *50g soft brown sugar*
- *3 x 20ml spoons golden syrup*
- *115g chocolate chips*

- *Preheat the oven to gas mark 5, 190C, 375F.*
- *Rub the butter or margarine into the flour, baking powder and bicarbonate of soda.*
- *Stir in the sugar, syrup and chocolate chips.*
- *Shape into small balls and arrange on a greased baking sheet.*
- *Flatten lightly. Bake for about 15 minutes until golden.*
- *Cool on wire rack.*

CHOCOLATE HIGHWAY

In September 2003, a tanker carrying liquid chocolate overturned and its cargo covered three lanes of the Pinheiros highway in Sao Paulo, Brazil. Brazilian media reported that children "stripped to their underwear ... covering themselves in chocolate."

SWEETS AND OTHER TREATS

HOW TO MELT CHOCOLATE

In a microwave. *Place coarsely chopped chocolate in a microwave-safe container and heat at medium power for 1 to 4 minutes, until the chocolate turns shiny. Remove from the microwave and stir the chocolate until completely melted. Stir milk and white chocolate after about 1 minute.*

In a double boiler. *Place chocolate pieces in the top of a double boiler or a heatproof bowl over hot, barely simmering, water. Melt the chocolate, stirring until smooth.*

CALORIE COUNT

A 45g milk chocolate bar has only 220 calories whereas a 55g serving of potato chips has 230 calories. Chocolate also contains vitamins A1, B1, B2, C, D and E as well as calcium, potassium, sodium and iron. A chocolate bar contains more calcium, protein and B2 vitamin than a banana or an orange.

THE BIGGEST CHOCOLATE BAR IN THE WORLD

The biggest chocolate bar in the world weighed more than 1985kg. It was the main attraction at the 15th International Milka Chocolate Festival on July 11, 1998 in the Austrian Alpine town of Bludenz. It measured 5 metres by 2 metres.

HOT CHOCOLATE SAUCE

Serves 4
- *240ml whipping cream*
- *175g dark chocolate*

- *Place the cream in a saucepan and heat to just below boiling.*
- *Break the chocolate into small pieces, add to the cream, reduce the heat and melt the chocolate, stirring frequently.*
- *Serve hot.*
- *Excellent with ice cream*

RICH CHOCOLATE TRUFFLES

- *150g dark chocolate, grated*
- *150ml double or whipping cream*
- *A small knob of unsalted butter*
- *Cocoa powder to coat*

- *Bring the chocolate and butter to room temperature.*
- *Warm a mixing bowl and place the chocolate in it.*
- *Heat the cream gently until just below boiling.*
- *Pour a quarter of the cream into the centre of the chocolate and mix it well.*
- *Add the rest of the cream a little at a time, working it in well.*
- *Blend in the butter.*
- *Cool the mixture overnight.*
- *Form into small balls and roll in cocoa powder.*
- *Eat within two days.*

WORLD'S BIGGEST EGG

The Belgian chocolate producer Guylian made a chocolate egg using 1950kg or 50,000 bars of chocolate. Twenty-six craftsmen worked for 525 hours to build the egg. The egg measured 8.32 metres high and beat the 1996 South African record. That egg was 7.65 metres high.

BRITISH EASTER BINGE

By far the best-selling Easter product is the Cadbury's creme egg, which outsells every other chocolate during the months from New Year's Day to Easter. Brits consume almost 300m creme eggs a year, making a 70% share of the market. Altogether we eat 80m full-size Easter eggs, together with boxed and other chocolates worth £440m.

CHOCOLATE FUDGE

- *450g plain chocolate*
- *60g unsalted butter*
- *345g tin of condensed milk*
- *1 x 2.5ml spoon vanilla essence*

- Break chocolate into pieces and put into a saucepan with the butter and condensed milk.
- Heat gently until melted and the mixture is smooth.
- Do not allow to boil.
- Take off the heat and beat in vanilla essence.
- Beat the mixture well for a few minutes until it thickens.
- Pour into tin and smooth out.
- Chill for a couple of hours until firm.
- Cut into squares to serve.

MARS RAID

A woman stunned staff at a north London branch of Woolworths when she bought more than 10,000 Mars bars and had them loaded into her chauffeur-driven limousine. She took every single one in stock - 10,656 of them packed in 220 boxes - and paid for them in cash with £50 notes. The total bill was £2,131.

SNICKERS

Franklin Mars invented the Snickers bar in 1930. Chocolate manufacturers currently use 40% of the world's almonds and 20% of the world's peanuts.

CHOCOLATE FRENCH TOAST

Serves 4
- *4 eggs*
- *250ml brown sugar*
- *100ml double cream*
- *250ml milk*
- *1 x 5ml spoon vanilla essence*
- *1 x 2.5ml spoon ground cinnamon*
- *pinch of ground nutmeg*
- *unsliced white loaf*
- *200g dark unsweetened chocolate, grated*
- *butter for frying*

- Preheat the oven to gas mark 4, 180C, 350F.
- Mix together the eggs, sugar, cream, milk, vanilla, cinnamon and nutmeg in a big bowl.
- Cut 4 thick slices of bread, slit them to make a pocket in the middle and fill this with chocolate.
- Soak the filled bread in the bowl with the egg mix for a minute.
- Fry them until golden brown.
- Put the chocolate toast on a baking tray and bake for about 10 minutes until the chocolate is melted.

REVEALING WHO YOU ARE

New Zealand psychotherapist Murray Langham believes chocolate preferences reveal people's personalities. Milk chocolate lovers tend to be innocent people who like to live in the past, while fans of dark chocolate are materialistic, problem solvers who are excited by the future. White chocolate aficionados have an innate sense of fairness and believe they have the power of the universe at their command.

NATIONAL PREFERENCES

According to the one writer "Chocolate in blue wrappers won't sell in Shanghai or Hong Kong because the Chinese associate blue with death. Neither Swiss nor Germans like girl pictures on their chocolate packages."

S'MORES

- *Graham Crackers or Rich Tea biscuits*
- *Marshmallows*
- *Plain chocolate bars*

- Traditional US treat which should be cooked on a campfire.
- Place a square of chocolate onto a biscuit.
- Place marshmallow on top of chocolate.
- Place another piece of chocolate on top of marshmallow and top with another biscuit.
- Microwave on medium until marshmallow begins to expand.
- Do not overcook.
- At a campfire roast marshmallow first.
- The warm marshmallow will melt the chocolate when squished together.

AMERICA'S FAVOURITE

Chocolate is America's favourite flavour. A recent survey revealed that 52% of U.S. adults said they like chocolate best. The second favourite flavour was a tie (at just 12% each) between berry flavours and vanilla.

DRINKS

APHRODISIAC

The Aztec Emperor Moctezuma is said to have consumed several goblets of 'xocolatl' before entering his harem, leading to the belief that it had aphrodisiac properties. Casanova also drank chocolate before bedding his conquests. They may both have been right as chemists have discovered that chocolate contains phenylethylamine, an amino acid which does have aphrodisiac properties.

BRAZILIAN HOT CHOCOLATE

Serves 2
- *125g dark chocolate, grated*
- *500ml milk*
- *50g Muscovado or dark brown sugar*
- *80-100ml espresso or strong black coffee*

- *Add the grated chocolate to the milk and heat it up gently until chocolate has dissolved.*
- *Then pour in the coffee and sugar and stir thoroughly. Serve immediately.*

CARIBBEAN HOT CHOCOLATE

Serves 2
- *125g dark chocolate, grated*
- *40g Muscovado or dark brown sugar*
- *½ egg yolk*
- *500ml milk*
- *½ vanilla pod*
- *½ cinnamon stick or 1 x 2.5ml spoon ground cinnamon*
- *a pinch of ground nutmeg*

- *Mix the grated chocolate, sugar, egg yolk and 100ml of the milk in a bowl.*
- *Split the vanilla pod and put it with the cinnamon and nutmeg in a saucepan with the rest of the milk and heat it.*
- *Remove pan from the heat and pour the chocolate mix into it and stir carefully until it thickens a little.*

DRINK FOR THE RICH

The high import duties on cocoa beans in England meant it was a drink only for the wealthy. London's first Chocolate House was opened in 1657 by a Frenchman, who described it as "an excellent West Indian drink." Samuel Pepys mentions his visits to chocolate houses: "Went to Mr Bland's and there drank my morning draft of chocollatte."

CHOCOLATE COFFEE

Serves 1
- *20ml brandy*
- *15ml dark creme de cacao*
- *15ml chocolate syrup*
- *120ml hot black coffee*
- *30ml milk*
- *whipped cream*
- *cocoa powder*

• *Heat ingredients gently and serve in a heated mug.*
• *Top with whipped cream and sprinkle with cocoa powder.*

EARLY ADDICTS

The 17th century Italian explorer, Antonio Carletti, commented on the people of cocoa producing regions, Spaniards, "and any other nationality" that drank cocoa: "once they start it they become so addicted that it is difficult for them not to drink it every morning, or late in the day ... or when on shipboard ... they carry it in boxes ... or made into tablets which dissolve quickly in water."

CHOCOLATE BANANA TODDY

Serves 1
- *15ml dark rum*
- *15ml creme de banana*
- *10ml dark creme de cacao*
- *150ml hot chocolate*
- *whipped cream*
- *nutmeg*

- *Combine rum, liqueurs and hot chocolate in a heated mug.*
- *Top with whipped cream and sprinkle with nutmeg.*

CHEF CREATES CHOCOLATE CURRY

A Birmingham chef has come up with a korma flavoured with chocolate and Asian spices. The chef, 37-year-old Iqbal Moin Hussain, told his local newspaper: "It took me about 20 attempts to get it right, but now it's perfect." But he warned that it was not an ideal choice for those watching their weight as it's crammed with cream.

SAVOURY DISHES

Using chocolate in savoury recipes may sound strange but it has a long tradition going back to the Aztecs – try it!

PEPPER-CRUSTED STEAKS

Serves 2
- *2 x 150g tender beef or venison steaks*
- *1 x 20ml spoon olive oil*
- *1-2 x 5ml spoons coarsely cracked black pepper*
- *salt to taste*

Sauce
- *1 x 20ml spoon olive oil*
- *1 x 20ml spoon shallots, finely chopped*
- *1 x 20ml spoon balsamic vinegar*
- *30ml port*
- *60ml beef stock*
- *1 x 5ml spoon chopped fresh rosemary*
- *15g unsweetened chocolate, coarsely chopped*

- Brush the steaks with the oil then season with salt and pepper, pressing it firmly into the meat.
- Heat the oil, add the shallots and cook 1 minute.
- Add the vinegar and port and reduce until syrupy.
- Add the stock and rosemary and bring to a simmer.
- Stir in the chocolate and cook until the sauce thickens slightly; keep warm on low heat.
- Grill the steaks as desired.
- Serve on a pool of the sauce with fresh, steamed vegetables.

CHOCOLATE SOLDIERS

In 1900 Queen Victoria sent specially made chocolate bars to soldiers fighting in the Boer War as a New Year's greeting. The Mars company invented M&M's for soldiers in World War II. American soldiers in the Gulf were sent modified chocolate bars which remain solid at temperatures up to 60C (140F).

IN THE NAVY

In 1825 the Navy bought more cocoa than the whole of the rest of Britain. It was considered the perfect drink for sailors on watch duty, being nutritious, hot and non-alcoholic. Amongst sailors in the Atlantic Ocean and the Baltic Sea the cold wind from the north-east was known as a 'chocolate gale.'

CHILLI CON CARNE CON CHOCOLADA

Serves 4
- *1kg onions, peeled and chopped*
- *oil for frying*
- *500g minced beef*
- *2 cloves garlic, peeled and crushed*
- *1 x 5ml spoon each of ground coriander, ground cumin, oregano*
- *2 large tins red kidney beans*
- *bottled chilli sauce – not chilli powder (to taste)*
- *110g sliced button mushrooms*
- *1 large tin tomatoes*
- *110g tin tomato purée*
- *275ml tarragon vinegar*
- *110g dark cooking chocolate, grated*

- *Preheat the oven to gas mark 4, 180C, 350F.*
- *Fry the onions in the oil in a large pan until golden, then drain into a deep, lidded ovenproof dish.*
- *Fry the mince, garlic and spices until browned, then mix in with the onions.*
- *Add beans and their liquid and the remaining ingredients, stir and cover with water.*
- *Cover dish and bake for 1½ hours.*
- *Even better if made the day before and reheated.*

"Don't wreck a sublime chocolate experience by feeling guilty. Chocolate isn't like premarital sex. It will not make you pregnant. And it always feels good."

Lora Brody,
author of Growing Up on
the Chocolate Diet